ROADS TO ROME

ROADS TO ROME

JOHN HESELTINE

FOREWORD BY COLIN FORD

FRANCES LINCOLN

To my wife, Flavia, and our children, Nathalie, Tara and Julian, who reluctantly stayed at home while I spent far too much time wandering around Italy.

Frances Lincoln Limited
4 Torriano Mews
Torriano Avenue
London NW5 2RZ

British Library Cataloguing in Publication Data
A catalogue record for this book is available from the British Library.

ISBN 0 7112 2552 4

Created, edited and designed for Frances Lincoln Ltd by Berry & Co (Publishing) Ltd
47 Crewys Road
London NW2 2AU

Designed by Anne Wilson

Printed in Singapore

9 8 7 6 5 4 3 2 1

HALF-TITLE PAGE: *Egnazia*
Horace recorded that on his journey along the Via Appia in 38 BC he passed through the city of Gnathia, where an old stretch of road is still visible at the important archaeological site now known as Egnazia.

TITLE PAGE: *Subasio*
A white road, once the ancient cartway to Spello, curves above the mist on Monte Subasio overlooking Assisi, an area rich in sacred and mystical associations.

ABOVE: *Via Flavia*
Like the all-seeing giant spectacles described in *The Great Gatsby*, this optometrist's sign keeps an eye on the Via Veneto area of Rome, just north of the vast Terme di Diocleziano.

CONTENTS

RIGHT: *Faenza*
As with most towns along its way, the Via Emilia used to
pass right through the centre of Faenza but with the rise in
the popularity of the car, traffic was redirected around the
edge of town on a new road bearing the ancient name.

FOREWORD: TAKE NOTHING BUT PICTURES

Rome, a grey, wintry day. Huddles of tourists, in raincoats and under umbrellas, are trying to comprehend the epic scale of the vast red and orange brick Roman Baths of Caracalla, an 1800 years' old leisure centre built to hold nearly 2,000 bathers at a time. Their guidebooks tell them that the infamous emperor Marcus Aurelius Antoninus (whose nickname "Caracalla" comes from the Gallic tunic he always wore), apparently granted Roman citizenship to every possible freeman in the Empire, solely so as to raise enough taxes to pay for the baths, and his other ambitious building projects.

In these gloomy conditions, however, it is difficult for even the liveliest imagination to visualize what Caracalla's baths were like in the days when one fourth-century Roman historian found them so mammoth that he compared them to provinces. Better to consult a nineteenth-century English writer, Bulwer Lytton:

> Imagine every entertainment for mind and body; enumerate all the gymnastic games our fathers invented; repeat all the books Italy and Greece have produced; suppose places for all these games, admirers for all these works; add to this, baths of the vastest size, the most complicated combination; intersperse the whole with gardens, with theatres, with porticoes, with schools; suppose, in one word, a city of the gods, composed but of palaces and public edifices, and you may form some faint idea of the glories of the great baths of Rome.

In a fold of the long ruined exterior walls of the Baths of Caracalla, which would once have towered 100 feet (35 metres) over his head, one man ignores both the drizzle and Byron's "arches upon arches" above him. Instead, he crouches down to aim his camera at a particularly weather-beaten, colourless patch of brick, through which the winds of centuries have eroded a jagged hole leading – well, leading nowhere really, except into shadow.

This is John Heseltine, English travel photographer, who has spent two decades taking pictures the length and breadth of Italy, building up a comprehensive library of images for books and magazines. When a commission is completed, or on one of his visits to do more personal work, he pores over maps of whatever area he is in, seeking out the remains of old Roman roads – some plain for all to see, some barely visible, some long buried. When he finds them, he makes the very personal and atmospheric black and white images that fill this book.

Heseltine's love affair with Italy is in a time-honoured tradition. From the eighteenth century on, the British have admired the art and taste of the classical world above all others, and no aristocrat's education was complete without taking the "Grand Tour". Its highlight was Italy, with its rich store of antiquities and ancient monuments. By the nineteenth century, Thackeray tells us:

> Every winter there is a gay and pleasant English colony in Rome, of course more or less remarkable for rank, fashion and agreeability, with every varying year. Thrown together every day, and night after night; flocking to the same picture galleries, statue

galleries, Pincian drives, and church functions, the English colonists at Rome perforce become intimate, in many cases friendly. They have an English library, where the various meets for the week are placarded: on such a day the Vatican galleries are open; the next is the feast of St. So-and-so; on Wednesday there will be music and vespers in the Sistine Chapel; on Thursday the Pope will bless the animals – sheep, horses, and what not; and flocks of English accordingly rush to witness the benediction of droves of donkeys. In a word, the ancient city of the Caesars, the august fanes of the Popes, with their splendour and ceremony, are all mapped out and arranged for English diversion.

This expatriate community naturally included artists. In the eighteenth century, Joshua Reynolds and Richard Wilson spent time working in Rome. In the nineteenth, so did Robert and Elizabeth Barratt Browning, Byron, Dickens, Walter Scott (who had a house in the city), Shelley and J.M.W. Turner, to name some of most celebrated. Keats famously went there to die, writing his own moving epitaph: "Here lies one whose name was writ in water."

In those days, before the invention of postcards, visitors who wanted souvenir pictures purchased them from local photographers. Pre-eminent among these in the 1850s were two Scotsmen, James Anderson – one of the many artists and photographers who congregated at the Caffè Greco, opposite the Spanish Steps – and Robert Macpherson. Macpherson opened his studio in 1851, and was soon being called the "foremost photographer in Rome", "gifted with that rare endowment, the art of pleasing". In Florence, in 1852, the Alinari brothers established what is now claimed to be the oldest photographic company in the world, with archives numbering over three and half million photographs. Later in the century, travellers like Sir Benjamin Stone, who was to found Britain's National Photographic Record, commissioned local photographers to take views, and then learned to do it for themselves.

Back in 2005, in the Baths of Caracalla, Heseltine shows me his latest photograph on the screen of his digital camera – no more waiting for film to be processed – before we start walking down the best-known Roman road of them all, the Via Appia. Our route is soon dominated by the tomb of Cecilia Metella. Byron was here, too, in the persona of Childe Harold:

> There is a stern round tower of other days,
> Firm as a fortress, with its fence of stone,
> Such as an army's baffled strength delays,
> Standing with half its battlements alone.

I have not brought Byron, nor Bulwer Lytton, nor Thackeray, as pocket companions on our trek, nor yet Wilkie Collins, Hawthorne or Trollope, all of whom walked this way. No, my altogether less well known and more matter-of-fact guide is Augustus Hare, prolific and opinionated nineteenth-century traveller who, in the 1860s and 1870s, published guidebooks to many European countries. I have had a sneaking affection for Hare ever since I learned that he went to the same Oxford college as I did; that, and the fact that he was always on the lookout for picture opportunities, makes him an especially apt gazetteer for an occasion like this.

Hare's *Walks in Rome*, which went into no less than eighteen editions in thirty-seven years, lists suggestions of "the best subjects for Artists who wish to draw at Rome, and have not much time to search for themselves. Many of these spots, however, have lost the great beauty which formerly distinguished them." One of the first things I realize about Heseltine is that he would be unlikely to agree. The beauty he seeks is not found in grand buildings, but in details, telling combinations of light and shade, textures and shapes, similarities and contrasts, ancient and modern, from which he can construct a picture, an impression, an abstract.

It may seem odd to call pictures of actual landscapes, street scenes, people and buildings abstract. But Heseltine's pictures do fit the definition – they are abstracted from real scenes. To see what I mean, I suggest you borrow a trick of the trade from the great Henri Cartier-Bresson. Turn the book upside down, and see how the photographs remain perfectly composed and coherent even when they are no longer recognizably realistic. Doing that may encourage you to study these beautiful black and white prints a bit longer. Having admired what you see on the surface, look beneath it. Photographs like these deserve to be given time.

Looking up our position in *Walks in Rome*, it seems that nothing has changed since Augustus Hare's day: "It is at this point that the charms of the

Via Appia really begin. A short distance farther, we emerge from the walls which have hitherto shut in the road on either side, and enjoy uninterrupted views over the green undulating Italian plain, strewn with its ruined tombs, castles, and villages, and long lines of aqueducts, to the Sabine and Alban mountains." Hare counsels walkers to keep their eyes open for "an ancient cloister and sculptured fountain, a mouldering fresco and medieval tomb, a mosaic crowned gateway or a palm shadowed garden".

"Mouldering" – precisely the kind of thing that makes Heseltine's eyes open wide. Most of the grand tombs lining the Via Appia, designed to impress passers-by with their dead occupants' achievements and wealth, were covered in expensive marble. Cecilia Metella's tomb still is. But, over the centuries, the marble on most of the others has either fallen off or been stolen. Our photographer likes it that way. Indeed, rather than show me the "Quo Vadis?" church where St Peter is supposed to have had a vision of Christ in AD 56 (see page 23), with Jesus' footprints "preserved" in a slab of white marble, Heseltine prefers to take me to what are claimed to be the "original" stone footprints. And every few yards we stop to admire the Roman lettering – no, lettering is too trivial a word – the calligraphy. Beautiful and always totally legible, it is perfect, unsurpassed in the centuries since it was carved (Santa Maria Capua Vetere, see page 36).

It is hardly surprising that our walk of only a few miles takes all day. Even under that grimly overcast sky, Heseltine's eyes are constantly darting into every nook and cranny. I once had a very different, yet strangely similar, experience in the company of the great Hungarian-born street photographer Andre Kertész. Different, because it was on the cacophonous streets of New York, where I had gone to interview the eighty-three-year-old in connection with an Arts Council exhibition in London. Similar, because he insisted on walking the two miles or so from the BBC's Rockefeller Center studio to his home in Washington Square. It took over three hours, not because Kertész was frail and slow-moving, but because he never stopped looking for, and pointing out to me, photographs – on the sidewalk, across the road, round corners, in shop windows, through doorways and inside taxis. It was, literally, an eye-opening experience.

Kertész was observing people, and the interactions between them, which he called "little happenings". For Heseltine, on the other hand, people are often secondary – they appear in only about a quarter of the pictures in this book. They need to fit into his composition, to be in exactly the right place at exactly the right time. Like, for instance, those marvellously positioned priests and their umbrellas in an otherwise deserted St Peter's Square (see page 148 and front cover); the silhouette at the bottom of the Vincoli staircase (see page 138); the old priest averting his gaze from the brazenly nude sculpture in San Marino (see page 113). Once, I watched Heseltine wait patiently for someone to walk into just the right spot in relation to a shadow and a stretch of wall, rather like the burly shopper in Faenza (see page 5).

Most of the time, Heseltine's eyes are searching bricks, stones, even the road beneath our feet – not for people then, but for the marks people have made. Where we are walking, the Via Appia follows the edge of a stream of volcanic lava and is "paved with little squares of lava that to tread over them is a penitential pilgrimage" (see pages 27 and 29). Music for our photographer's eyes. The music in Heseltine's *ears* was probably not Respighi's triumphal procession of legions returning from successful battles (in *Pines of Rome*). Nor yet Alex North's Oscar-nominated score for that old Hollywood version of the war against Spartacus, which ended – in real life as well as on screen – with the corpses of six thousand slaves hanging for mile after mile along both sides of the Appian Way.

But there *is* something musical about Heseltine's pictures, especially his studies of brick, stone and shadow. They evoke the very response Alfred Stieglitz was hoping for when he showed his photographs of clouds, his so-called "Equivalents", to the composer Ernest Bloch: "Music! Music! Man, why that is music!"

To look again at the pictures taken that grey February day transports me at once back to Rome and the Appian Way. Indeed, I can open this book almost anywhere and believe I was there – though I was not. This power to evoke so vivid a sense of place is a tribute to the truthfulness of Heseltine's photography, and gives one hope that at least one of his avowed aims – to ensure that future generations can see what Italy was like at the turn of the twentieth and twenty-first centuries – will succeed.

Ruskin, after all, wrote *The Stones of Venice* in the 1850s because he was convinced that that this "Paradise of Cities" would sink beneath the waters of the lagoon before his century was out. A hundred and fifty years later, Venice is still there. Heseltine believes he has observed a growing interest among Italians in preserving their heritage: perhaps it will ensure that those relics of the Roman Empire which have survived thus far will be there for a few more millennia.

The society which built and used the Roman roads has long gone. Walking that atmospheric ancient roadway, passing the baths, the equally huge chariot racing arena, and all the other once ostentatious architectural tributes to wealth and pleasure, one is acutely aware of trampling on the remains of a dead civilization, a civilization which was sowing the seeds of its own demise even while it was building: "The habits of luxury and inertia which were accentuated by the magnificent baths of the Emperors were among the causes of the decline of Rome."

Heseltine's evocative pictures underline the wisdom of the advice one sometimes sees displayed at heritage sites: "Take nothing but pictures". But, over the centuries, the British – and others – have mercilessly plundered antiquity: Roman booty can be seen in many of our stately homes. Even Augustus Hare built mosaics from the Palace of Commodus (on our stretch of the Appian Way) into his house in Sussex. Preferring my souvenirs to be photographic, I am more than happy to let Heseltine's beautiful black and white shadows of the distant and recent past powerfully summon up the great Roman roads of Italy, the materials with which they were built, and the men and women who have used them – and continue to do so.

In these pictures, ghosts really do come to life.

Colin Ford
March 2005

ROADS TO ROME

INTRODUCTION

The photographs in this project describe a series of photographic journeys around modern Italy using the early Roman roads that every young child learns about at school. Here the most modern expressions of twenty-first-century life are played out against an ancient Roman backdrop. When you travel on these old roads, many marked with modern signs bearing the ancient names, you feel a sense of travelling in years as well as miles. All the main cities linked by these roads are rich in history and culture, but the old routes also take the traveller through intensely interesting smaller settlements, as well as the seductive landscapes romanticized by advertising agencies and travel companies. Some of them seem little affected by the two millennia that have passed since ancient road-builders bridged these lands.

The arteries are as expansive as the Roman Empire itself, which built straight paths to access its far-flung conquests and received back through this early information superhighway the rewards of power, wealth and cultural diversity. This book is not a guide to instruct the traveller every step of the way, but instead forms a visual expression of the journeys that have been made and are still made on these straight passageways through space and time. It is an attempt to explore visually some of the essence of this rich, vital and complex nation, and some of the disparate connections that link the North to the South, the old to the new: the art of the ancient road-builder now expressed in neat slices of time divided by smooth shutter blades.

Ponte Taro
A newer Mercedes than the one I describe above rushes across the Ponte Taro on the Via Emilia just outside Parma, where pilgrims once stayed on their way along the Francigena route. The present bridge across the River Taro was rebuilt by order of Maria Louisa, the Austrian Duchess of Parma.

My own journeys through these roads began in the summer of 1970 when hitch-hiking eastwards from London. I had planned a relatively straight-forward route, crossing France, Germany and Italy and on to Yugoslavia and beyond. This would have been simple with the luxury of a train ticket, but was fraught with difficulties when thumbing lifts. France and Germany were relatively easy, but the Italians didn't seem to like the look of me and passed me by in large numbers. One of the major lulls in my progress happened near Milan, as the *carabinieri* removed me from the entrance to the *autostrada* for the umpteenth time. Rescue came in the form of a white Mercedes Benz 230SL, driven by Sophia Loren (or her double). She scooped me and my wretched rucksack off the approach road and bombed off in the direction of Brescia, waving her family snaps at me in the hot 90-mph wind that whipped over the open car. "Nobody else would ever have given you a ride," she laughed. At that moment I started to love Italy.

Since then, I have travelled around the country regularly, usually getting about by hire car and photographing places and things for numerous books and magazines about all things Italian. But the roads gradually became an interest in their own right and seem now to provide a unity for my own personal expression of what I feel the place was, and is, like.

I have sought to create a collective sense of place, as far as one can sum up a varied and sophisticated nation in a few photographic images. I thought I would have to make many extra sorties to illustrate various sections of the route, until I realized that I had already been along virtually every mile and the roads had become a natural map of my personal vision of Italy. Sometimes consciously, sometimes not, I had already tried to put into images what I saw and felt as I went on these adventures into the interior of Italy. And yet, as with all journeys, the more you find out, the less you feel you know; the more you see, the less you feel you have truly seen.

THE ROADS

To help hold the vast empire together, the Romans built a highly advanced system of roads. People had built roads long before Roman times. By about 1000 BC the Chinese had begun to construct roadways between their major cities. The Persians built a similar road network during the fifth century BC. But most of these early inter-city links were little more than tracks; it was the Romans who constructed the first extensive system of paved roads. Most of the well-known Roman roads were named after the Consuls who supervised their construction and they generally measured 16 to 20 feet (5 to 6 metres) wide and 3 to 6 feet (0.9 to 1.8 metres) thick. Several layers of crushed stone and gravel provided a base for the surface, which was paved with stone blocks, fitted close together without the need for mortar, and usually finished with compacted gravel, fashioned to a curve to allow water to run off. Milestones were erected and usually recorded the name of the emperor responsible. These were men like Claudius, Domitian and Trajan, who supervised road building with such authority and care that these same roads remain one of the most enduring legacies of the Roman Empire.

The Romans used their roads to transport troops and military supplies as well as to form a major communications link between Rome and its provinces. By the second century AD, more than 50,000 miles (80,000 kilometres) of paved roads connected Rome to almost every part of its Empire. Roman coaches even had a device attached to the wheels to measure the distance covered and 30 to 50 miles (50 to 80 kilometres) a day was considered to be an average journey. Government and military officials travelled by state mail carriage known as the *cursus publicus,* hauled by up to eight mules and stopping off at regular intervals for food and rest.

However, during the fourth century AD, Germanic tribes conquered most of the Roman territories in western Europe. With the decline of the Empire, the majority of Roman roads slowly fell into ruin and, during the following centuries, many became little more than drovers' tracks. In the years following the Renaissance, when road-building and repair once again received attention, Pope Gregory XIII, perhaps acknowledging the role the roads had played in the dissemination of Christianity, authorized the construction of routes that would accommodate more modern coaches, and a system of inns was established along the way. In 1580 the French philosopher Montaigne described his journey through Italy and the innkeepers who came out on horseback to meet carriages in order to persuade them to stay at their abodes where "Dining rooms are unknown: the windows are large and have no glass. If one closes the big wooden shutters to keep out the sun or the wind, then at the same time one also shuts out the light." One hundred and fifty years later things weren't much better, as Charles De Brosses confirms in his travel journal: "I have to speak ill of the road from Siena to Rome. It is vile, most vile and in itself bad enough to make every traveller despair."

There are many Roman roads throughout Italy and, indeed throughout Europe, the Middle East and Africa, but the routes in this book have been chosen to illustrate the cultural diversity that still exists within Italy and allows the traveller to start a journey in a modern, urban, high-tech, sophisticated "designer" environment and travel a hundred miles or so into areas of relatively unchanged landscape, where some crops are still harvested using age-old methods and where strangers are regarded with curiosity or even suspicion. In this way they offer an insight into the fusion of old and new that gives Italy its distinctive character, and provide a natural framework for a photographic account of its varied regions. Moreover, the roads themselves and the beauty of their stones, as well as the topographical and archaeological features along their way, are objects of fascination in their

Cobbles with sky
Many of the ancient basalt stones of the Via Appia became deeply rutted by the endless passage of wheels, and they were often covered with nineteenth-century cobbles and later coated with modern road markings. Under heavy traffic the newer stones are now themselves crumbling, creating a ragged patchwork of roadbuilding history.

own right. They opened up the Roman Empire to the East just as now they offer us a link with the distant past, always with the beckoning call of Rome echoing in the traveller's ears as, directly or indirectly, all roads eventually converge on the "Eternal City".

The roads have come to represent the recent past, as well as distant history, and many Italians still have an emotional attachment to these routes that perhaps harks back to family holidays, weekend outings, or something more tangible like the Lancia cars or Fellini films of the 1950s and 1960s, or to a memory of an age when the car was less of a dominating force in the landscape. In the foreword to his novel *The Garden of the Finzi-Continis*, Giorgio Bassani wistfully recalls a typical weekend outing along the Via Aurelia in 1957. The journey was one that they felt was a natural thing to do – to leave Rome for a day "without anything very definite in mind" – and it seems that this particular excursion, taking in the Etruscan tombs of Cerveteri, had a cathartic effect and produced the impetus to write of the Finzi-Contini family in Ferrara and of the oppressive period of Jewish history in the years leading up to the Second World War.

Quite definite themes emerge after following these roads: regional disparity, changing values, Italians' paradoxical love of their surroundings with their frequent disregard for environment, a modern youthful designer generation living against a stage-set of ancient Italy, quite conscious of all that went before. The modern matrix of ancient routes offers some certainty within the changing complexity of modern Italy and its close links to its history. Intriguingly, it was this network that enabled the Romans to create a unified Roman Empire in Europe and beyond, but now that circle is closing again and another Europeanizing movement is developing, much to the concern of many Italians. We see the old face of Italy under threat from Brussels, the world of mass tourism and globalized markets that bring McDonald's wrappers even to the canals of Venice.

In developing these themes, one senses that concern for environmental issues is growing in Italy and can be seen in such things as the rise of the national park movement in its protection of large expanses of unspoilt landscape, the closure of city centres to cars, and the "Slow Food" movement as a reflection of a "Slow Life" movement. However, large areas of less well preserved countryside can cause dismay to visitors not used to viewing the landscape in a utilitarian, functional sort of way. Ugly expanses of derelict concrete industrial buildings are frequently seen, as are pile of rubbish strewn along the roadside. Some families go for a drive in the country taking their rubbish with them to toss out of the window at the first opportunity. The intense pride Italians have for their country and their commune is not always matched with a pride in the local scenery. Perhaps such a blot on the landscape is considered superficial and unimportant in the context of the thousands of years that man has managed the land of the Italian peninsula, which is often treated more as a working environment and not something to consider for its own sake.

In urban areas the changes are equally obvious. The background to ancient sites is often a haze of pollution or smudges of dark smoke spoiling the deep azure sky. Distant views of large cities like Genoa or Naples are frequently obscured by a blanket of smog-like pollution and nearly every city, however elegant its *centro storico*, has a contrasting area at its perimeter where satanic factories and refineries belch out smoke and fire, a testament to the success of post-war industrialization. However, every nation has to produce wealth somehow and it should not surprise the culture pilgrims that Italy cannot survive only as a museum. Many Roman roads, as they approach town centres or even in the central piazzas themselves, are now packed with American fast-food eateries with the result that the ancient monuments are decorated with a confetti of old burger wrappers. Nevertheless, none of this manages to overwhelm the strong character of Italian towns, whatever their size. The old buildings, monuments, family shops, market places and restaurants are highly valued and Italians would not want to see changes of the order that have taken place in small-town America or in the English high street, where chain stores predominate and the multinational brand is king. Whether or not successive generations of Italians can ensure the survival of the distinctive features of their land is a matter of concern to many.

The Roman roads also long served as pilgrim paths, and here we see another aspect of the changing face of Italy. Religion was one of the certainties that bound together the fabric of Italian society, but a loss of interest on the part of young people, together with a crisis in the Catholic priesthood, means that fewer people are entering either the Church as a profession or churches as visitors. There are still plenty of men in black but they all tend to be older men. This is in marked contrast to the years after the world wars – look at a photograph of a town then and most of the priests are young. There are now very few young priests to be seen.

The landscape itself is also undergoing profound yet subtle changes. The structure of Roman roads extends into relatively remote parts such as Basilicata and Puglia in the far south. Now the state routes are being replaced by wide *autostrade* with enormous bridges and the extension of communications that can be seen in the rise of regional airports and the influence of the internet means that regional characteristics are in danger of being eroded. A noticeable change is that young people don't want to work at rural jobs any more and so rural crafts are beginning to disappear. For the tasks that have to be done manually, farmers need to source labour from Eastern Europe. At the same time, there is an increase in modern farming practices involving mechanization of everything from hay cutting and baling to harvesting grapes and olive picking. Brussels has also forced changes in traditional rural working practices so that many small producers find it is no longer possible to sell eggs or to use their time-honoured ways of making salami or cheese. Few Italians would disagree that their country is undergoing a profound transformation. I hope that these photographs offer both reminders of the rapid march of history and hints of the new Italy that is emerging.

John Heseltine,
March 2005

Bologna
The church of San Petronio in Piazza Maggiore was originally planned to be larger than St Peter's in Rome and the decision to scale down the design can be seen in parts of the exterior elevations. The upper façade was left unfinished but the lower façade is ornately decorated and affords seating, making it a popular place for a quick lunch, despite critical clerical glances.

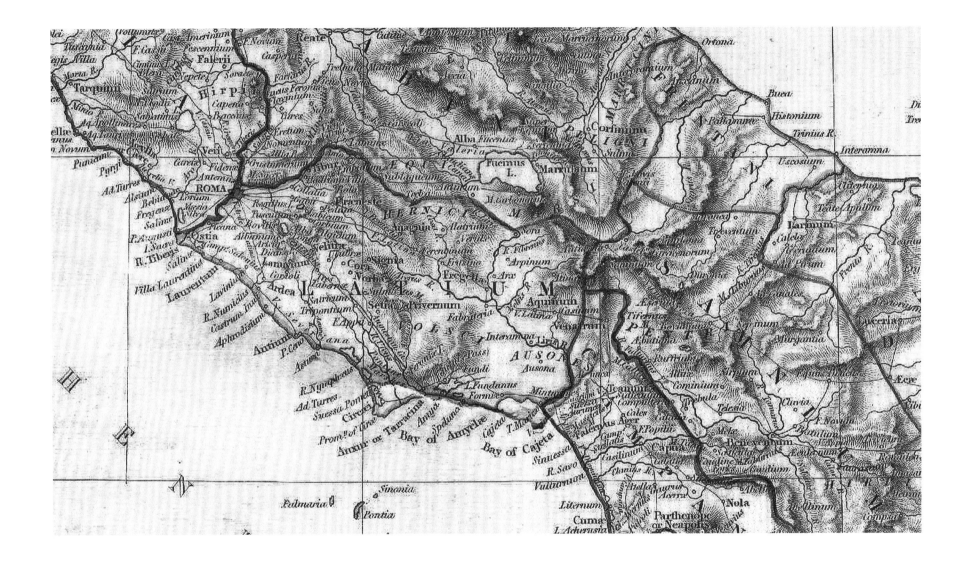

VIA APPIA

ROME TO BENEVENTO

AS THE ROUTE LEAVES ROME, HEADING SOUTHEAST, it passes the famous Baths of Caracalla before exiting the city walls through Porta San Sebastiano. From here it is a short distance to the church of Domine Quo Vadis?, San Sebastiano church and catacombs and on to the area now designated the Via Appia Park, where there are many impressive reminders of the road's importance. Once clear of the city, the road crosses the Colle Albano, passing Genzano, Nemi, Velletri and the Pontine Marshes before meeting the Lazio coastline near the rocky promontory of Monte Circeo. It then passes Gaeta, Terracina, Capua, nearby Montecassino and Caserta before reaching Benevento.

The Via Appia, the "Queen of Roads", extended from Rome to the great port of Brindisi, thus eventually linking the Eternal City with the Orient. Begun by Censor Appius Claudius in 312 BC, it provided a fast link to the eastern stretches of the Roman Empire, an expressway for the legions of soldiers who policed the hallowed territories. Constructed to a width of just over 13 feet (4 metres), it allowed two carriages to pass one another. The Emperor Claudius ordered that roads should be built to last forever; a close inspection of the stones used for the construction shows that the road builders took this decree seriously.

The original route, abandoned in the Middle Ages, headed southwards out of the city, but today it is a precarious walk along the first stretch of the Appia Antica: the narrow road is often busy with speeding traffic thundering along the cobbled surface and, as there are high, overgrown walls on either side, there is nowhere to walk safely. Beyond the well preserved Arco di Druso, where cars regularly queue for the traffic lights ahead, the road passes

through the ancient walls of Rome at Porta San Sebastiano and, after a further unremarkable kilometre of wing mirrors brushing rapidly past, the Appia Antica arrives at the church of Domine Quo Vadis?, so named because it was supposedly at this point that Saint Peter met Jesus leaving Rome and uttered the famous words, "Domine, Quo Vadis?" Inside the church, the footsteps of Christ are imprinted in white marble, a copy of an "original" impression housed in the church of San Sebastiano. Beyond here many travellers stop to visit the catacombs of San Callisto and San Sebastiano, from where the walker catches the first glimpse of one of the most imposing monuments on the Appian Way, the tomb of Cecilia Metella dating back to the first century BC. This was originally covered with earth but in medieval times it was converted into a fortified castle and palace as part of a larger fortified citadel that was built around this stretch of the Appia.

A little further on, a fine stretch of original Appian pavement is revealed, flanked by a rich array of tombs, buildings and fragments. In the mid-nineteenth century this area was recovered from obscurity and the archaeological relics arranged much as they are today. In his *Pictures of Italy*, published in 1888, Charles Dickens described the area vividly: "We wandered out upon the Appian Way, and then went on, through miles of ruined tombs and broken walls, with here and there a desolate and uninhabited house: past the Circus of Romulus, where the course of the chariots, the stations of the judges, competitors, and spectators, are yet as plainly to be seen as in old time: past the tomb of Cecilia Metella: past all enclosure, hedge, or stake, wall or fence: away upon the open Campagna, where on that side of Rome, nothing is to be beheld but Ruin. Except where the distant Apennines bound the view upon the left, the whole wide prospect is one field of ruin. Broken aqueducts, left in the most picturesque and beautiful clusters of arches; broken temples; broken tombs. A desert of decay, sombre and desolate beyond all expression; and with a history in every stone that strews the ground."

Here, so close to the centre of both modern and ancient Rome, just a few kilometres from Ciampino airport, the hard Fascist architectural expression at the Esposizione Universale di Roma (EUR), and the Colosseum itself, you experience a classic stretch of ancient road paved with smooth basalt rock from the Alban Hills just further south. After a cluster of imposing modern villas, stretches of original surface can still be seen, along with fragments and monuments. Here, the pedestrianized route becomes an archaeological promenade with fine examples of the original paving passing a succession of tombs, many – for example the Fusco and the Rabirii tombs – recently restored. These are just two among plentiful examples of reconstructed funerary monuments that are common here.

When I first came here twenty years ago it was late afternoon and the atmosphere was positively seedy; the ladies of the night took up their stations behind the tombs, and the ground was littered with discarded bottles, cans, condoms and hypodermic needles. Since then it seems as if a team of landscape gardeners has tidied the place and the cloak of dense foliage that acted like a curtain to the evening activities has been cleared away. Rubbish bins bearing the Appia Park logos appear every hundred metres and the restored tombs, many newly damp-proofed and rendered, have smart stone markers to indicate the family name. To be buried along the Via Appia was an ambition for Roman patricians and, before the tombs were stripped of their marble and allowed to fall down, this section of the road must have resembled a remarkable city of the dead.

Once clear of Rome the route heads towards the Alban Hills, passing the cleared Pontine marshland around Latina. As the road heads towards the coast, a Roman canal runs parallel with it. Once at the sea you find Monte

Caracalla
The huge walls of the Baths of Caracalla reach up to 100 feet (35 metres) in height and seem to belong to geology as much as architecture. Opened in AD 216, they provided a dramatic beginning to the Via Appia as it left the south of Rome.

Circeo, an evocative spot with both an elemental natural beauty and Roman ruins, and the supposed location of the Isle of Circe, which Homer's Odysseus was held in thrall by the enchantress. As the road passed through Terracina, it exited through the Porta del Sole (or Gate of the Sun), long considered the gateway to the South. In AD 109, Trajan ordered the rocky promontory of Pesco Montano to be cut away to allow the road to follow the coast, rather than diverting inland to Itri as had previously been necessary. This was no mean feat without modern machinery, as you appreciate when you stand at the foot of this massive rock and gaze upwards, imagining how it was done. The smooth cut faces have long offered a surface for graffiti artists and the messages themselves represent layers of time. If you look hard, you might spot scrubbed-off Fascist slogans overlaid with football expressionism.

From here, the builders of the ruler-straight Via Appia had to twist and turn with the contours of the landscape as it climbed eastwards from the town, passing the Temple of Jove (or Giove Anxur), built in the first century BC on a commanding site with views up and down the coast. All that remains of the main temple now is the long, arcaded foundations that once supported the 190-foot (60-metre) building, but this is impressive enough in its own right. Staring along the series of arches is like peering through infinite vaults of time and, with just the wind and the sea for company, it is easy to be transported back through the centuries to a period of pagan worship.

Just inland lies Montecassino, a Benedictine Abbey dating back to the sixth century AD and once an important seat of learning. Now it is better known for the great battle that waged there in the Second World War, when Allied forces dislodged the Germans from their stronghold at the cost of the Abbey buildings and some thirty thousandtroops.

More ghosts linger on the route to modern Capua, built around the ancient city of Santa Maria Capua Vetere, where Spartacus led his slave revolt. Indeed, it was eventually along this road that six thousand of his followers were crucified on the order of Crassus in AD 71. The area around Capua is not the most beautiful in the land, but the archaeological site – the second largest amphitheatre in Italy – is certainly impressive .

Passing through Caserta and close by Naples with brooding Vesuvius in the background, the road then reached Benevento with its magnificent Trajan's Arch.

Horti Scipionum
On the first stretch of the narrow Via Appia near the Porta Sebastiano the traffic hurtles past at high speed and there is less pedestrian space than on the New Jersey Turnpike. Behind this wall lies the tomb of the important Scipiones family and next door a small garden offers an escape for the modern gladiators of the road.

Church of Domine Quo Vadis?
It was supposedly at this point that Saint Peter
had a vision of meeting Jesus leaving Rome and
uttered the famous words "Domine, Quo Vadis?".
Now only rush hour traffic passes the doorstep
of the church named after the famous encounter.

Inside the Cecilia Metella tomb
Near the third milestone from Rome, intricate
layers of brickwork echo the passage of time as the
tomb became a fortress-cum-palazzo, then a ruin
and now a museum containing some of the finest
statues discovered on the Via Appia.

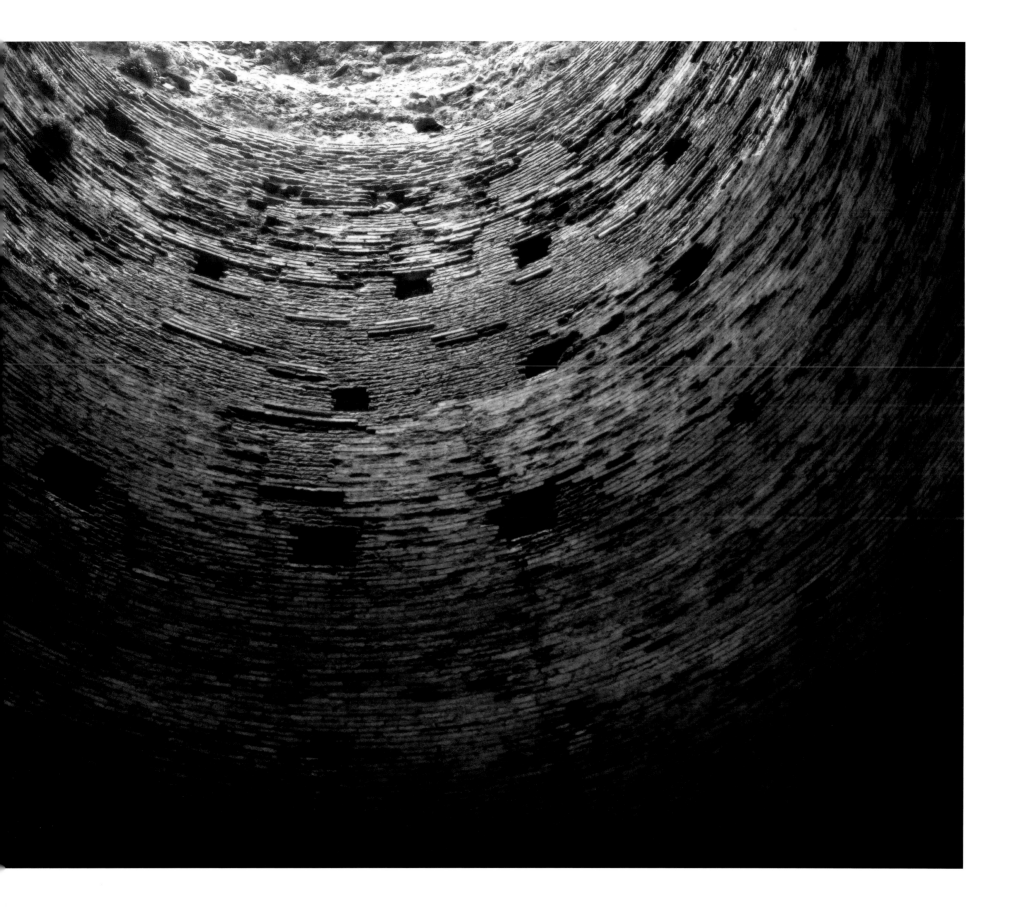

Via Appia, Rome
The most interesting section of the Via Appia
Antica, now designated an "archaeological
promenade" takes the walker over a long stretch
of original surface, surrounded by tombs and
framed by umbrella pines. Since becoming a park
in the late 1990s, the area has been tidied up and
lost some of its sinister reputation as a centre for
unsavoury nocturnal activities.

Military Zone

A solitary heroic figure graces a tomb that once stood in front of a romantic wooded background near "mile four", one of the many places where newly-weds were regularly photographed along the Appia Antica. Since the recent clean-up of the Appian Park the perimeter fence of an old military academy is revealed in all its glory.

Porta Napoli, Terracina
Also known as the Porta del Sole, or Gate of the
Sun, this was considered the gateway to the South.
In AD 109, Trajan ordered the rocky promontory
of Pesco Montano to be cut away to allow the road
to follow the coast. The smooth cut stone faces
have long offered a surface for graffiti artists and
the messages themselves represent layers of time.

Temple of Jove
As it passed through Terracina, the Via Appia
passed the Temple of Jove, or Giove Anxur,
built in the first century BC. All that remains of
the main temple now is the long arcaded
foundations that once supported the 190-foot
(60-metre) long building.

Vespa people carrier, Gaeta

Although it is now against the law, it is not
unusual to see an entire unhelmeted family
astride a scooter, especially in the South. In
Gaeta, south of Rome, three generations happily
move off oblivious to the fine details of the
modern law-maker. They pass two weathered
marble lions that still sit resolutely in their
transformed urban surroundings. The way in
which such ancient stones blend with the
modern environment, exposing layers of
archaeological history, is part of Italy's fascination.

Capua Vetere
The ancient city of Capua is known as Santa
Maria Capua Vetere to distinguish it from the
unattractive modern city which now bears the
noble name. Once you are within the
impressive archaeological site – the second
largest amphitheatre in Italy – you might level
your gaze below the smoke-smudged skyline
and imagine the cries of horror echoing from
the massive walls of the subterranean
passageways where many a man and beast
passed on their way to meet their doom.

Piazza Spaccanapoli

This Greek allegorical figure depicting the Nile was found headless and half buried by the debris of time. It was moved to this spot near the Largo Corpo di Napoli and erected on a plinth, dignified with a head in 1657, and now provides a timeless backdrop to the stalls of street traders and other actors on the Neapolitan stage.

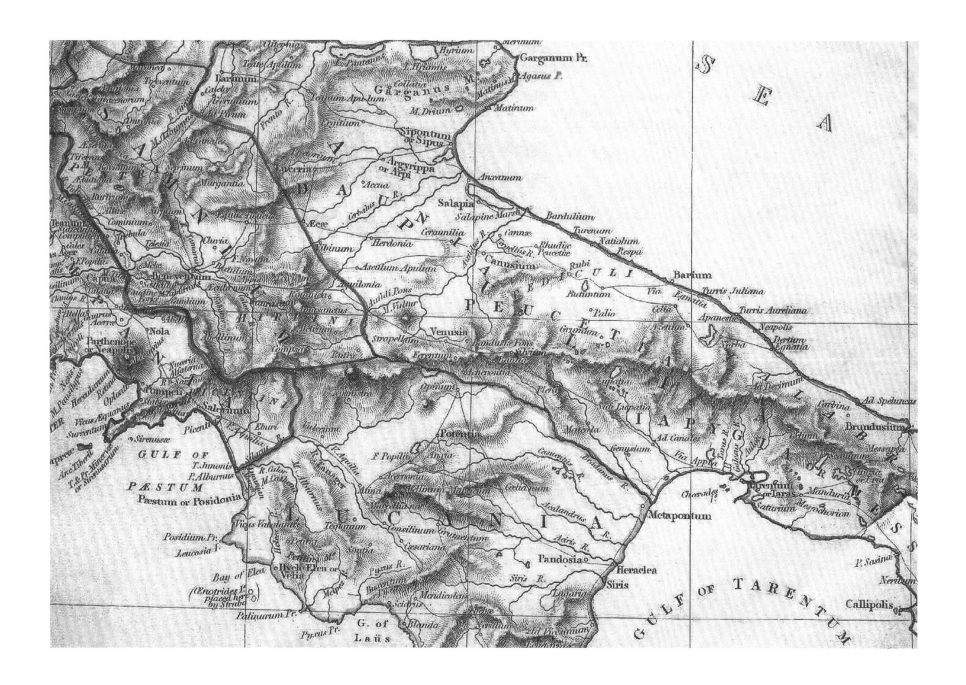

VIA APPIA

THE SOUTHERN ROUTES
FROM BENEVENTO TO BRINDISI

AT BENEVENTO the road forks, leading in one direction to the southern leg of the road from Rome and in the other along a later route, the Via Appia Traina. The continuation of the main route traverses Campania into the parched landscape of Basilicata around Tricarico, Miglionico and Matera. Skirting the coast near Taranto in Puglia the route crosses the narrow heel of Italy to reach its destination at Brindisi on the Adriatic coast. The Appia Traina crosses the Apennines to reach Anzano and continues through Lucera, Canosa, Andria, Ruvo, Terlizzi, Bitonto, Bari, Polignano, Egnazia, Monopoli and Torre Canne. Just further inland lies the famous Trulli area around Alberobello and Locorontondo. The road passes the whitewashed town of Ostuni before reaching the ancient port of Brindisi, where the Roman world made its bridgehead with the Orient.

The poor dry Mezzogiorno landscape of Basilicata area was made famous by the film of Carlo Levi's book *Christ Stopped at Eboli*. Once the preserve of poverty, disease and death, the Sassi area of Matera is now undergoing something of a transformation. These were once crude dwellings hewn out of the bare rock, eerily reminiscent of the burial chambers of the necropolis that can be seen in the distant cliffs – how strange that life should mimic death so clearly. Gradually many developed more elaborate architectural features and even a number of churches were built. However extensive the embellishments to the dwellings, at the end of the day the inhabitants remained susceptible to malaria and tuberculosis, and an early death. After hundreds of years of settlement, they were relocated to more modern accommodation and the area was virtually uninhabited until the 1970s, when people started to take a renewed interest in these unusual homes and a slow programme of modernization began. Now the transition from poverty to chic is in full swing, with holiday homes, nightlife, and at least one "hip" hotel gentrifying the Sassi area.

The Italian way of dealing with rubbish is a dispiriting sight, especially further south where the route of the "Queen of Highways" resembles a municipal dump on a busy day. This problem is nothing new: ever since Roman times rubbish of unimaginable variety has been dumped anywhere on city streets or country roads. The abandoned beds and sofas are taken advantage of by the large numbers of prostitutes, who have their own uses for the Roman byways. In contrast, a rather more pleasing sight is the graphic patterns of ploughed fields, etched in muted tones of brown and gold, or the sight of the distinctive hay rick still common around here and a reminder of the proximity of simple agrarian values. Roman soldiers travelling along the southern reaches of the Via Appia may have passed thousands of these tidy cones. The art of assembling hay ricks, now a vanishing one, was once a source of local pride and each region still has a different way of arranging hay to dry. However, the age of mechanization and a diminishing interest in rural work in general has spelt the impending demise of such regional diversities. In many parts of Italy, only Eastern European labourers now work on the land, so perhaps Croatian haystack designs will start to appear!

This is a hard landscape and, even in late spring, the background is often barren and parched and sometimes yields little at all to the farmers so dependent upon the bounty of God's earth. Carlo Levi describes spring in Basilicata as having "none of the stir of renewed life, none of the budding and tumescence of the happy lands of the north . . . A vital part of the revolving year was missing and its absence saddened the heart."

Bombed in the Second World War, the modern city of Taranto is now surrounded by naval dockyards and heavy industry. It has given its name to the tarantula spider and to the frenzied dance and music that were meant to cure the madness its poison produced. A more modern dance, the tarantella, continues the tradition. The Romans founded the important citadel of Tarentum nearby. Modern industry has now ruined the environment here. The water is murky and the trees look unwell, while the city itself has a reputation for crime, drugs and more than the occasional murder.

Via Appia Traina, built around 108 BC, is the northern leg of the Appian Way, built later to extend access to the port of Bari. The road was built upon an even earlier one, the Via Minucia, and is supposedly the route followed by Horace on his legendary journey from Rome to Brindisi in 38 BC. Passing Canosa and Santa Margarita, both with remarkable churches, the route traces the Puglian coast until, just inland, it passes near the site of the battle of Cannae, where Hannibal famously ambushed and defeated the Romans in 216 BC. Now an archaeological park, it is a lonely, quiet place full of ruined buildings and architectural fragments, some bearing Roman inscriptions. A superb section of the original road is preserved further on at Egnazia, where you can see the limestone blocks that once paved the entire route of the Appia Traina, built in the first century BC to connect Benevento with Brindisi. It was through this latter port that exotic eastern goods and culture found their way to Rome. These days the place is a riot of signs pointing to ticket offices where travellers can buy ferry tickets to Greece, but the stretch of coast here is also the destination of the more sinister trafficking of people trying to enter Europe illegally from Albania and North Africa. Both southern legs of the Via Appia arrived here in great ceremony but nowadays the landmark that for centuries marked the end of the Appian Way is a sorry sight. There used to be two marble columns to dignify this spot, but one collapsed in the sixteenth century and was reconstructed in Lecce. The famous single column that remained has since been taken away for lengthy restoration, leaving only a rusty metal barrier and the column's graffiti-covered plinth to mark the historic spot.

Villa Cimbrone
From the belvedere of the Villa Cimbrone, perched high above the Amalfi Coast, the weathered profile of a statue peers wistfully towards the east. This relatively inaccessible part of Campania was popular with Romans and has long relied on the proximity of the Via Appia to connect it to Rome and the rest of Italy.

Farmer

The friendliness of Puglian people is well
known, but in many older faces we can see
features from the distant past. This noble face
could belong to any of the countless invaders
who have left their mark on this land, from the
Greeks, Romans and Byzantines to the
Normans, Spanish and Swabians.

Vanishing point
The ruler-straight lines of the original Roman roads can be seen at many places along the Via Appia. Here in the Matera province the summer heat takes early afternoon temperatures well over 40°C (104°F). Wisely, most people stay indoors and sleep off lunch.

Sassi dwellings in Matera, Basilicata
The Sassi area has long fascinated film
directors, most recently Mel Gibson, who
created an impression of ancient Jerusalem here
for *The Passion of the Christ*. Soon after this
production, the inhabitants of Matera, who were
looking forward to a further boost to local tourism,
were instead visited by a plague of locusts, which
drove away travellers and ravaged local agriculture.
Such is the fickle hand of fate.

Chiesa del Purgatorio, Matera
While the poor huddled in wretched caves in
the Sassi area, the wealthy built fine palaces
and churches in the upper part of town. The
weathered Baroque façade betrays the ravages
of time as a priest places a heavy iron key in
the ancient door, either to lock the poor out or
to protect the spirit within.

Hay rick
The vanishing art of assembling hay ricks was once a source of local pride, and each region still has a different way of arranging hay to dry. But the age of mechanization and a diminishing interest in rural work have spelt the impending demise of such regional diversities.

Trulli cat
The remarkable conical houses, known as *trulli*,
had symbols painted on the roofs to ward off evil
spirits so the residents could sleep at night, even
if a black cat happened to pass their doorstep at
full moon on the thirteenth day of the month.

VIA APPIA: THE SOUTHERN ROUTES FROM BENEVENTO TO BRINDISI

Taranto from the Parco delle Remembranze
The Mare Piccolo, a lagoon surrounding the east
side of the ancient Spartan city of Taras, is largely
given over to oyster cultivation, an activity that
has continued since Greek times. The Romans
founded the important citadel of Tarentum near
here; heavily bombed in the Second World War,
it later developed a successful heavy industry
which has clearly left its grubby mark on the
local environment.

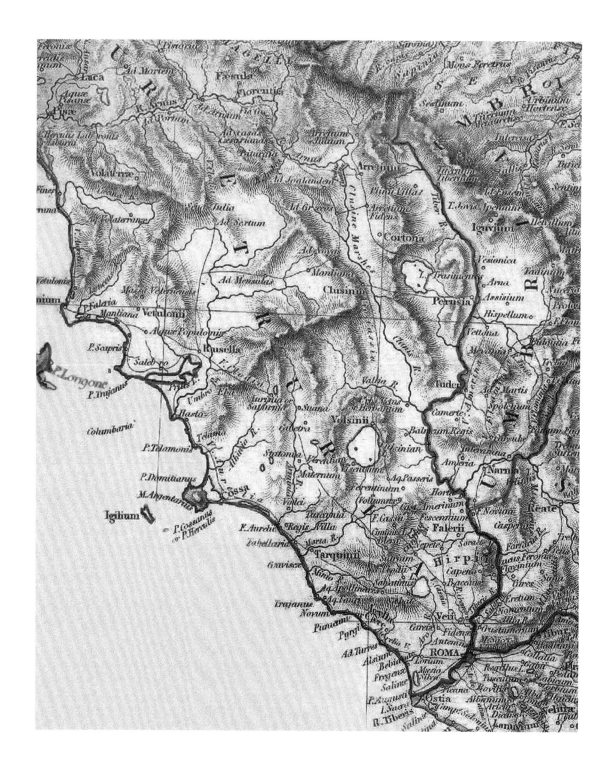

VIA CASSIA
ROME TO FLORENCE

As the via cassia leaves Rome from the Ponte Milvio, it passes by the ancient Etruscan city of Veio and crosses some fine parts of Lazio including the lakes of Bracciano, Vico and Bolsena, and the ancient city of Viterbo. Entering Tuscany it navigates the beautiful landscape around San Quirico d'Orcia and Pienza, skirting the great vineyards of Montalcino and Montepulciano before entering Siena. From here it passes near other wonderful Tuscan towns like San Gimignano and Volterra as it winds its way to complete the journey to Florence.

Originally an ancient Etruscan route, this road was named after the Proconsul Cassio Longino Ravilla, who supervised much of its construction between the years 117 and 107 BC. It starts off by sharing the exit route from Rome with the great Via Flaminia, crossing the Tiber at Ponte Milvio, but, after the river, the ancient Roman North–South highway heads due north to bring together a complex of roads that link Rome with the central and northern cities. It crosses a large part of Lazio, passing the volcanic crater now filled by Lago di Bracciano, and begins its path into the heart of Etruria, starting with the area around Viterbo and Lago di Bolsena.

This route has many literary references, in part because of the enduring popularity of its fabulous towns and cities but also because of the long fascination that writers have had with Etruscan culture in general. Just over the border with Umbria at Orvieto, the Duomo's façade displays wonderful Etruscan visions of hell re-created by Renaissance hands. Every town in the area seems to have a museum displaying the relics of this civilization and a host of signs along the Via Cassia points you to tombs and other historical sites. In *Etruscan Places*, D.H. Lawrence spoke of "a queer stillness and a curious peaceful repose about the Etruscan places" and this is still something the traveller might notice in a place like Veio, north of Rome, or in Chiusi, just in Tuscany, where the area abounds with tombs.

Beyond, the road winds through the spectacular landscape that was once home to this lost civilization. Above Siena and just west of the Via Cassia lies the beautiful ancient Etruscan town of San Gimignano, its famous skyline bristling with medieval towers; a little further west is the equally impressive town of Volterra. Both places possess a certain magic out of season and walking the streets of San Gimignano in the darkening winter evening you sense ghosts of the past moving silently before you. Henry James described the place as "some rare silvery shell, washed up by the sea of time, cracked and battered and dishonoured". Of course, any sense of enchantment quickly vanishes as spring approaches and tourists start to arrive in force, when one is reminded of another of James' descriptions of the place, likening its heritage to "the driest and most scattered bones, producing the miracle of resurrection" and "the buried hero himself waking up to show you his bones for a fee, and almost capering about in his appeal to your attention. What has become of the soul of San Gimignano who shall say?"

A century earlier, in his *Italian Journey,* Goethe wrote about his rushed passage along this route. Racing – in the other direction, from Florence to Rome, in a desperate bid to get there as soon as possible – he represented a new generation of travellers who were beginning to use the ancient roads that were slowly being repaired and promising a new lease of life.

Ever since the Renaissance, Florence has laid its spell on countless visitors and we now see the well preserved monuments decorated with young people from all over Europe, China, Japan and America, anxious to photograph one another against the background of, perhaps, the Loggia dei Lanzi.

Ponte Milvio
The Ponte Milvio used to carry both the Via Flaminia and the Via Cassia across the Tiber and it was reputed to be the scene of the great battle when Constantine, after receiving a vision near this spot, took control of Rome and converted the city to Christianity. In the late 1930s a new bridge was begun to carry the Via Flaminia away from the city in Fascist triumphal style but it wasn't opened to traffic until 1951.

Anguillara
Dramatically sited on the edge of the volcanic lake
of Bracciano, the small fishing village of Anguillara
lies just west of the Cassia, only 15 miles (25
kilometres) from Rome, yet a world away in time.

Fountain of the Giants
Pope Pius V granted Villa Lante, in modern-day Lazio, to Cardinal Gambera in 1566 and the great architect of the time, Vignola, was commissioned to design hydraulic confections in stone to amuse seventeenth-century guests who wandered the grounds and dined out among the extravagant fountains. The huge statues here represented the rivers Tiber and Arno, symbolizing the strong relationship between the papacy in Rome and the Medici in Florence.

Orvieto

At the heart of the ancient Etruscan civilization,
Orvieto is a beautiful city perched high upon a
commanding tufa outcrop. Walking through the
narrow medieval streets you suddenly come across
the amazing fourteenth-century cathedral which
took over a century to build.

Water diviner
Using just a twig and a pocket watch, skilled
Umbrian water diviner Luigi Venturini is
regularly relied upon to locate good water supplies
for even the most ambitious construction projects.

Siena priests
This procession of men of the cloth gives little indication of the crisis that exists within the Catholic Church. Racked by unsavoury scandals and neglected by an increasingly secular age, the priesthood is no longer a popular choice of career and there is now a huge shortage of priests in Italy, which is being partly met by attracting novices from Africa, the Philippines and other far-flung dioceses.

San Gimignano ghosts
The town of San Gimignano was supposedly
settled by the followers of the Silvio group,
following the Catalan conspiracy in Rome, but
its buildings now give little away about the
intervening years and at night the streets could
belong to any period in Tuscan history. Here, a
group of nuns hurrying home seems to vanish
into the glare of modern sodium lighting.

Oltrarno street scene
Oltrarno – literally, the other bank of the River
Arno – feels very different from the city centre on
the opposite side of the river. This scene typifies
how everyday encounters are constantly being
enacted, regardless of the surroundings, so that
sometimes Italy seems like a great theatrical set,
providing a magical backdrop to the generations of
players that stalk its stage.

Loggia dei Lanzi
Benvenuto Cellini's sixteenth-century statue of *Perseus Beheading Medusa* was intended to signal a warning to Cosimo 1's enemies and give them an inkling of their likely fate. Giambologna's *Rape of the Sabine Women*, to the far right, adds a further note of impending violence.

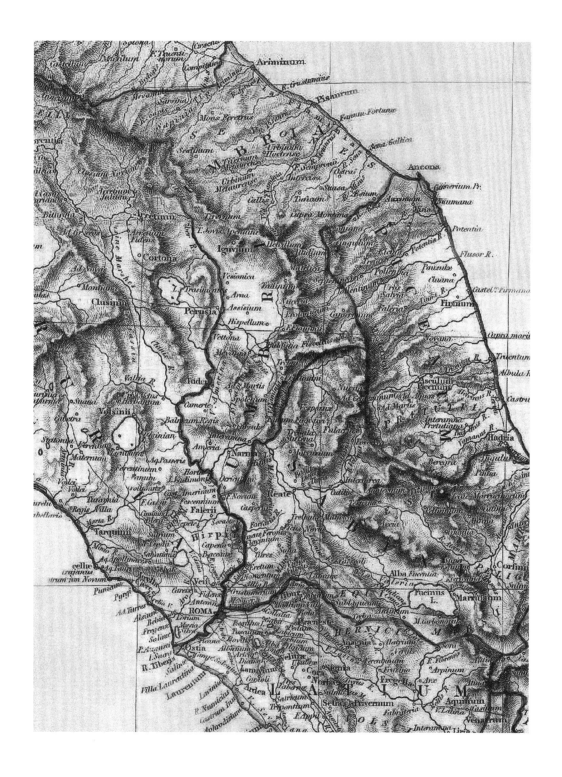

ROADS TO ROME

VIA FLAMINIA
ROME TO FANO

R OME'S FAMOUS CORSO, the Marcus Aurelius Column, the Piazza del Popolo, Ara Pacis and Porta Flaminia all line this majestic route's exodus from the city. Out of town, original sections of pavement can be seen at Otricoli and the bridge at Narni. Like the Via Appia, this route evolved into two distinct sections: the eastern route, or Flaminia Nuova, visits the lovely Umbrian towns of Terni and Spoleto and Trevi. The main route, or Flaminia Vecchia, passes the well preserved Roman remains of Carsulae as well as such beautiful places as Montefalco, Bevagna, Spello, Assisi, the Gola del Furlo and nearby Urbino before reaching Fano, where it was linked to Rimini and the Via Emilia.

The Via Flaminia is actually a complex structure of routes that crossed the centre of Italy to link Rome to the Adriatic coast to the north-west. Commenced by Censor Caius Flaminius before his death in the Battle of Trasimeno in 217 BC, it leaves Rome from the Piazzale Flaminio just near the Porta del Popolo, crossing the Milvian Bridge over the Tiber where, in AD 312, Constantine the Great supposedly received a portent of his victory over the larger army of Maxentius the following day and vowed to convert to Christianity. In the late 1930s, a new bridge, the Ponte Flaminia, was begun to create a triumphal entry into the north of the city but was not opened until 1951.

The road travels a fairly unremarkable route for the first few miles, passing strange towns like Rignano Flaminio, so close to Rome and yet feeling so remote. Things begin to look more promising as you cross the border into Umbria and reach the famous Roman bridge at Narni, where the Via Flaminia used to cross the River Nar at the impressive height of around 130 feet (40 metres). The massive structure was rebuilt by Augustus but only a small part of it now remains alongside its modern replacement. Just north is one of the most important sites on the Flaminia: the ruined Roman town of Carsulae, where an old stretch of the original road winds its way right through the middle of town, passing well defined Roman ruins of a forum, temples, a theatre, a triumphal arch, along with several more ordinary houses and shops, all surrounded by attractive landscape. While the modern Via Flaminia carries a heavy load of traffic every day, surprisingly few tourists seem to bother to stop at Carsulae, the handful of visitors seemingly more aroused by rituals of courtship than any fervent interest in archaeology.

Beyond lie splendid towns like Todi, Spoleto, Trevi, Montefalco, Bevagna, Spello, and, a little further west, Assisi and the heart of Umbria and Italy as a whole, and Lake Trasimeno. Here is the place where Flaminius met his appointment with destiny. At dusk, a soft, misty light often descends upon the shores of Lake Trasimeno, investing the scene with a wistful, melancholy air. However, this mood is nothing to the gloom that descended upon the Roman army camped beside the lake at Tuoro one spring day in 217 BC. Consul Flaminius thought he was in pursuit of Hannibal and his Carthaginian army when in fact they were surrounded. As the Romans moved off in the morning mist they were attacked on all sides by Hannibal's men and driven down to the lakeside where a huge part of the 25,000-strong Roman army was massacred, along with the reinforcements that followed. The pink light often seen here at evening is a reminder of the local legend which recalls that so much blood flowed into the river after the battle that it was renamed Sanguineto.

North of Foligno, the Via Flaminia becomes less busy and passes through a landscape near Valtopina where country folk guard their secret truffle grounds jealously. Along this stretch of the road, traces of the old Roman road frequently appear alongside the modern replacement, an example being the Ponte Mallio near Cagli, an ancient bridge built with massive stones. Thought to be very early Roman or even older, it is known locally as the Etruscan Bridge. An alternative spur of the Flaminia takes a detour to Urbino but the main route heads east, passing an interesting section of elevated Roman viaduct near San Vincenzo and skirting the impressive Gola di Furlo. Here, the modern traveller enters the Roman tunnel named after Vespasian, its entrance marked by Latin inscriptions and still proving itself just about capable of coping with the modern volume of traffic. There are more places where you can glimpse original bridges and section of pavement can be clearly seen at Fossombrone, but, as you head towards the coast, there is little to link the present route with its illustrious past. However, the town of Fano on the coast is still built around the original Roman grid plan and there is a copy of a milestone that recorded the distance to Rome (195 Roman miles), but otherwise the atmosphere here is of a very busy summer resort, slightly melancholy out of season. The coastal road turns northwest and passes Pesaro before reaching Rimini and the beginning of the Via Emilia.

Filling station ruins
Once beyond the Porta Flaminia, there is little of architectural note before the Tiber, but on every street corner the Via Flaminia's name is prominently displayed, even though this area of Rome has some seedy parts and a frequent sense of abandonment.

Rignano statues (overleaf)
Rignano feels like a long way from anywhere but is, in fact, little more than a half-hour's drive from Rome. Here the Flaminia passes the doorstep of a mason's yard that now stands silent but still displays weathered mythical and biblical figures, bird baths, mock columns and garden ornaments.

ROADS TO ROME

Carsulae lovers
Two lovers embrace in a circular tomb on the
northern edge of the ancient ruined city of
Carsulae. To the right is the Porta Damiano
through which the Roman road once passed
on its way straight through the middle of town.

Subasio track
Italy has a huge network of white roads that criss-cross the landscape, some traversing large distances. Here the gravel track seems to extend indefinitely, only bounded by the Umbrian fog as it winds its way from the Via Flaminia, which circles Monte Subasio before dropping down into Assisi.

Trasimeno Pier
Lake Trasimeno lies at the heart of Umbria and,
indeed, Italy. In the wistful light of dusk, it is easy
to recall the gruesome end of Consul Flaminius,
founder of the road that still bears his name. On
the north side of the lake, he and his army were
destroyed by Hannibal in 217 BC.

Via Ritorta
West of the Via Flaminia lies Perugia, once an important Etruscan city. The ancient heart of Umbria's principal city seems to have changed little since medieval times.

Fano beach
Fanum Fortunae, or Fano as it is now known, was the veritable end of the road and marked the spot where the main route of the Via Flaminia met the Adriatic coast. Once the site of the Roman Temple of Fortune, the Arco di Augusto is now the only substantial monument left to recall the Roman origins of the place that Augustus established as a colony here around 10 BC. Robert Browning stayed here but these days the visitors tend to be package tourists attracted by the expansive beaches. The temporary nature of the beach architecture contrasts with the massive stones one passes along the way from Rome.

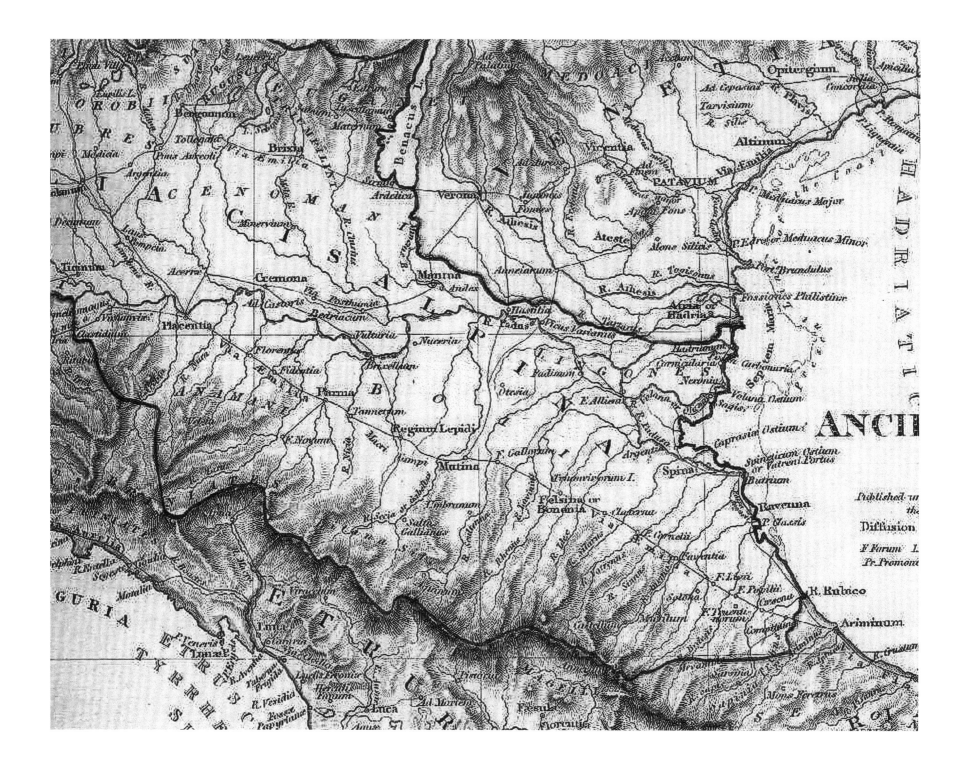

ROADS TO ROME

VIA EMILIA
MILAN TO RIMINI

A T MILAN (Mediolanum) the Via Emilia begins its route to Rimini on the east coast, where it joins the Via Flaminia to connect with Rome. From the Apennines in the west it follows the Po Valley through Piacenza, Parma, Reggio Emilia, Modena, Bologna, Imola and Faenza before reaching the Adriatic coast. The route provides access to the tiny hilltop Republic of San Marino.

This road was built around 187 BC by Consul Marcus Aemilius Lepidus to connect Rimini on the Adriatic coast with Milan, 200 miles (320 kilometres) to the north-west. Later, in medieval times, it became an important pilgrim's route to Rome as well as to Ravenna and Venice. A modern route still runs in its path, following the Po Valley to the Apennines, and many of the original bridges still remain. The road eventually gave its name to the papal state of Emilia, which, in turn, was joined with its neighbour after the unification of Italy to become Emilia Romagna. On maps of Northern Italy this dead-straight route resembles a textbook example of a Roman road: a straight line with way-stations regularly spaced along its length. The towns that now link the Via Emilia began as small settlements or mansions consisting of a main building surrounded by taverns. These developed into *vici*, or small villages, which grew into towns. And what settlements these have become – many of the most sophisticated cultural centres in Italy: Piacenza, Parma, Reggio Emilia, Modena, Bologna and Faenza are all still wonderful places and the Roman road passes right through their centres. Slightly off the actual road lie Cremona, Mantua, Ferrara and Ravenna, all of which owed a good part of their development to the completion of this route. Travelling through these towns you can experience some of the highlights of ancient Italian architecture as well as very best of modern Italian food and design. This is an area where a successful blend of craft and manufacturing carries on against a background landscape that is still essentially agricultural, even if some of the farmers do drive Lamborghini tractors.

In between the towns, the landscape of this part of Emilia Romagna is unrelentingly flat and largely featureless, except for regular glimpses of farmhouses, irrigation ditches and stands of regularly spaced birch trees. Frequently even these dissolve into obscurity as the regular fogs of the Po delta creep across the territory, blinding all sight and muffling all sound. I have been driven through these eerily blank spaces at frightening speeds with the view ahead limited to just a few metres and the local driver relying on the straightness of the roads, certain that his satellite navigation system will alert him to dangers ahead. The road's destination is Rimini, once the important Roman colony of Ariminum, where the Via Emilia and the Via Flaminia met, and now a popular seaside resort. It is also the main route to the tiny Republic of San Marino.

San Lorenzo Maggiore, Milan
A statue of Constantine, apparently robbed
of his umbrella, stands with sixteen Roman
columns, a reminder that this area was once
the centre of Mediolanum, a vital strategic
outpost of the Roman Empire. The statue
commemorates the AD 313 Edict of Milan,
which established Christianity as the unifying
religion of the Empire.

Birches, Mantua Province (overleaf)
Plantations like this are seen all over central Italy,
but, however modern they may be, walking
through them at dusk gives one an eerie sense
of timelessness.

ROADS TO ROME

Landscape in snow
A solitary figure walks along a side road off the Via Emilia, leaving the small town of Cella near Reggio nell' Emilia. The staked fruit trees create graphic patterns in the frozen landscape at the foot of the Apennines.

Suburbscape in rain
The town of Parma has a superb modern centre,
but as in most Italian towns – indeed most
European towns – the outskirts are an
unpromising assembly of industrial estates, fast
food places, filling stations and unattractive
signage. This stretch of the Emilia suggests little
of the architectural marvels of Parma's baptistry
and duomo or of the high standard of living its
residents enjoy.

VIA EMILIA: MILAN TO RIMINI

Bologna arcades
Handsome porticoes and 22 miles (35 kilometres)
of arcades built out of mellow brick dominate the
old centre of Bologna; there is a reassuring feeling
of permanence to the unspoilt city centre.

Torre degli Asinelli, Bologna
The twelfth-century tower affords a wonderful view
of the city from its 318-foot (97-metre) summit,
which is reached by 500 steps periodically
illuminated by small windows. This is one of a pair
of towers, the other being the Torre Pendente, but
in the twelfth century the skyline of Bologna bristled
with around 200 such towers.

Baker

The staff of this large bakery in Ferrara clock in at 3 a.m. to ensure a plentiful supply by morning of fresh bread, crostini, and the town's distinctive *copia* for both its shop and the local restaurants. These skilled workers are all in their mid-seventies. In the twenty-first century, no young people are prepared to work such unsociable hours.

GENITORI SPOSA

FIGLI FRATELLO

INCONSOLABILI

D. M. PP

Hebrew cemetery, Ferrara
The melancholy atmosphere of the Ghetto in Ferrara is intensified by a visit to the cemetery near the city walls, where the dead vastly outnumber the living Jewish population. Here Giorgio Bassani is buried, and among the shadowy tombs it is easy to re-create the end of his wistful tale *The Garden of the Finzi-Continis.*

San Marino priest
This elderly priest in San Marino gives a wide
berth to the modernist rendition of the female
form as he slowly makes his way along the quiet
wintry pavement to church. Ironically, Europe's
oldest republic was founded by St Marinus, a
fourth-century monk and stone-mason.

VIA EMILIA: MILAN TO RIMINI

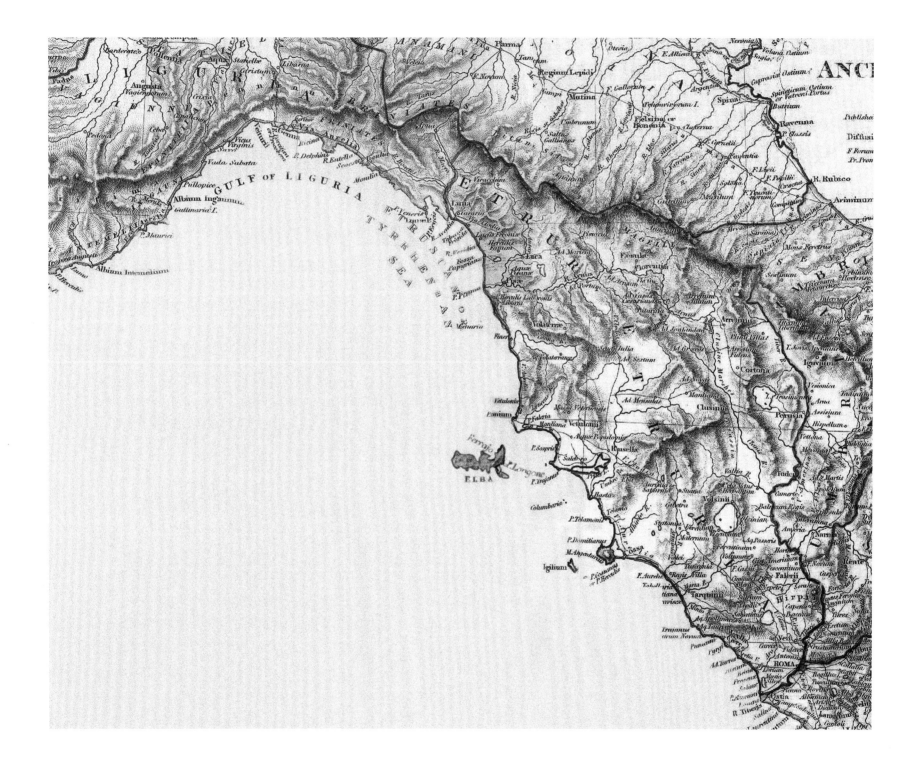

VIA AURELIA
ROME TO VENTIMIGLIA

THIS ROUTE LEAVES ROME through the Porta Aurelia, passing near the Forum Boarium. Cerveteri is the first notable stop with its amazing Etruscan necropolis, with remains also to be seen around Citavecchia and Tarquinia. There is a detour from the north–south path which makes a circular tour of Tuscany, taking in Pisa and Lucca before returning to the coast near Viareggio, passing the mountains around Carrara and entering Liguria, where it skirts the famous Cinque Terre as well as Genoa, Albenga, San Remo and Ventimiglia. Here an extension provided access to the Roman cities of Provence and, further on, to Spain, passing the valuable silver mines to finally reach Cadiz.

This mainly coastal route traverses a long part of the west and north-west seaboard of Italy and takes the modern traveller through a wide range of regional diversity. Its beginning and end is the Forum Boarium around the Piazza Bocca della Verità; from here it crosses the Tiber and passes close by the Vatican on its way north-west towards the coast. The first coastal station was at Palo, or Alsium, where the remains of a large Roman villa have been discovered. At Cerveteri, once one of the richest and largest of Etruscan cities, there are well-preserved burial chambers in the necropolis. The first settlement here dates back to the tenth century BC and at its heyday the town covered a large area and controlled the coast up to Monte Argentario. Further Etruscan and Roman sites are scattered all the way up this stretch of coast, but probably the best known are at Tarquinia, which has an important necropolis.

The ancient site of Cosa, close to Orbetello and Monte Argentario, was the original destination of the Aurelian Way until it gradually became extended to Genoa and beyond. Skirting the Maremma Park the road passes through modern Grosseto before arriving at the Etruscan centres of Vetulonia and Populonia on the coast close to the modern embarkation point for the island of Elba. At Livorno the road passes the Roman harbour that was transformed by the Medici, and much of this sixteenth-century fabric can still be appreciated. However, it is dwarfed by the sprawling modern facilities with huge collections of goods coming and going against a demonic backdrop of refinery chimneys.

Just after Pisa the route makes a curve inland to the beautiful city of Lucca and back to the coast at Viareggio, where some modern Italians find paradise and others a holiday nightmare. The original road become harder to trace and the modern autostrada bearing the same name beckons the driver in a hurry. Here, the backdrop to the Aurelian Way becomes the Alpi Apuane, the colossal mountain range around Carrara where Michelangelo once walked to find his seams of perfect marble.

North of here you get a glimpse from the modern Aurelia of the huge grubby sprawl of Genoa, which does not look its best from this viewpoint. Further west, the Ligurian Riviera gradually become less developed and sections of the old road appear between Alassio and Albenga, offering atmospheric places to walk, passing seldom-visited Roman burial complexes with sections of paved road disappearing through the wooded hills above the sparkling Mediterranean. Here it is generally known as the Via Augusta, after the Emperor who extended the Aurelia to the French border and beyond. There is not a lot left to see, the dust of ancient buildings and bones having been long scattered by the winds. At Laigueglia, most locals, when asked for directions to the old Roman road, seemed not to believe that it existed anywhere near this seaside town. I was about to abandon my quest when I came across an unprepossessing track that led to a stretch of what is now clearly marked as the Via Augusta: I was begining to develop a nose for Roman dust. From the old stones of the Aurelia you frequently catch sight of the impressive elevated sections of the autostrada that has adopted the name and now rushes heavy traffic over the steep Ligurian hills covered with hothouses and vines. The last important Roman site before crossing the border is on the east side of Ventimiglia, where, among unattractive surroundings, the visitor can find the remains of a Roman theatre standing right next to an incredibly busy stretch of road that has been built right on top of the old route.

Livorno cars
The port at Livorno was developed by the Medici and much of the old harbour still remains, but the expansive modern replacement was a target for Allied bombers in the Second World War. Since then Livorno has been rebuilt to become one of Italy's largest ports.

Aqueduct (overleaf)
Almost as important as the roads themselves, the structures that carried vital water supplies can still be seen in several parts of Italy, here near the ancient settlements around Citavecchia.

ROADS TO ROME

Paradiso
A lonely tanker skirts the Tuscan coast, passing between the Three Stars and Paradise on its way to Genoa. Meanwhile, Viareggio's holiday stage-set awaits another summer fantasy.

Pisa

Twenty years ago the area around Pisa had many
derelict factories, warehouses and mills, many of
which have since been pulled down to make way
for a wave of new industrial parks, with their
buildings finished in dark glass, polished metal
and primary colours.

Alpi Apuane
The Lago di Vagli is a hydroelectric basin created in the 1940s when the small village of Fabbriche di Careggine was flooded. At low water you can see the church tower and every ten years the lake is drained for maintenance and the ghostly ruins of the village are revealed. They are often visited by the families of evacuated artisans, as well as by curious tourists.

Carrara

Michelangelo wandered these mountains to find
seams of perfect marble to do justice to his art,
and it was here that Brunelleschi sought the ideal
materials for his dome in Florence, only to see the
ship carrying the precious cargo sink near Pisa.
Marble has been excavated from these mountains
for centuries to produce fine buildings, floors,
tables and funerary memorials, but only by visiting
the quarries do you understand the difficulties the
early quarriers must have faced before the advent
of automated cutting and transport methods.

Genoa lion

It may look unprepossessing from a distance, but Genoa has a beautiful old centre, which includes this nineteenth-century lion patiently guarding the steps leading up to the black-and-white-striped Duomo of San Lorenzo. The Doumo itself is far older, dating back to the twelfth and thirteenth centuries.

No more dancing
An abandoned dance hall north of the Aurelia near
Liguria's border with Piedmont no longer echoes
to the sound of a dance band; its boarded-up doors
and windows are unlikely ever again to glow with
the twinkling lights of evening pleasure.

ROADS TO ROME

Taggia bridge
Known locally as the Roman bridge, the 16-span,
850-foot (260-metre) pedestrian bridge across
the Argentina River is actually Romanesque.
It nevertheless provides a graphic contrast to the
elevated Via Aurelia autostrada in the background.

Graffiti

Even the graffiti can be read as a manuscript
of the past, as layers of time recall lovers, bored
youths, druggies, tourists, bikers, hikers and
priests who have wandered past this empty
church on the Via Augusta, perched above the
coast near Albenga.

Riva Liguria
Once a stopping-off point for Romans travelling to Gaul, Riva is now a quiet and slightly down-at-heel seaside resort on the Via Aurelia.

ROME

T IS NOT POSSIBLE to make a full visual account of the "Eternal City" in a chapter. Indeed as Goethe wrote in *Italian Journey*, "To take in even a small part of everything there is to see here would take a lifetime or, rather, the lifetime of many human beings learning from each other in turn." Romans themselves take for granted the pages of history that are represented everywhere in stone. Carlo Levi, in an essay on the Roman people, wrote, "Here, everything has already existed: and existence has not vanished into memory, rather it has remained present, in the houses, the stones, the people: a remarkable welter of times and differing conditions that resolves into an absolute simplicity of emotion and interest. It has all been done before: only death is still to come." All the humble photographer can do is present a few images, themselves constructed by selecting brief moments in time, and hope they both suggest the feeling of timelessness a visitor encounters here and evoke the strong sense of place that the city imparts.

Located at the very heart of Roman antiquity, the Golden Milestone in the Forum was the monument that marked the spot where all roads began and ended. The stone itself is no longer there and, like many artefacts of the period, has been scattered, reassembled and copied, but the original base can still be seen in place in the Forum and is a reminder of the huge numbers of roads that converged on this "mile zero" spot. The Romans used old fragments in their own building – the Arch of Constantine's reliefs, for instance, were taken from earlier pagan monuments. Today we marvel at how these glorious Roman structures could themselves have crumbled into ruins and how recently the place has been recovered from obscurity. It is incredible to think of the hallowed stones of the Temple of Vesta lying under layers of mud and debris, with cows grazing above. The Temple was one of the most sacred sites in Rome and housed the Eternal Flame, tended by the Vestal Virgins and symbolizing the perpetuity of the Roman state, but it wasn't until the 1930s that it was reassembled from fragments that had been scattered around the Forum. The smooth creamy marble pavement of the Via Sacra as it passes the hallowed Temple of Vesta reminds us again of the importance of roads, but here the journey is more a spiritual one than a mundane means of terrestrial transport.

The way in which fragments of Roman civilization have been reassembled, rearranged and recycled into other buildings is something that is seen all over Rome. Not far from the oldest Roman market, the Forum Boarium, dating back to the years of the Republic, is the Casa Manilio, named after its humanist owner, Lorenzo Manilio, who built this town house in 1468 and decorated it with architectural fragments he collected from the ancients sites of the city; the layers of time are further complicated by engraved Latin and Greek texts that look as though they were also plundered from classical ruins but which were, in fact, contemporary references to the owner. The cyclical movement of time coming around again is seen everywhere in the city, especially at the Campidoglio, once the grand centre of the Roman Empire, but then deteriorating to the point of becoming a goat farm before being resuscitated during the Renaissance. Michelangelo remodelled the Campidoglio by excavating areas of the Forum to find suitable classical statuary on which to base his Renaissance blend of sixteenth-century elegance and the vestiges of Imperial Rome. The fusion of ancient and modern is even to be spotted on the manhole covers, drainpipes and city street-cleaning machines, all of which proudly display the letters SPQR, a reference to Senatus Populusque Romanus, the original local government administered from the Capitol. In Rome, the Dark Ages were indeed a time of obscurity. We are fortunate to live in an age that values the past – even if that is sometimes to the point of overzealous respect.

And everywhere in Rome there are men of the cloth, people praying or intent upon the business of prayer management, solemnly going about Church matters and ecclesiastical bureaucracy. The Colonnade that encircles the Piazza San Pietro has recently taken on the appearance of an airport check-in area, with X-ray machines, metal detectors and fearsome guards scrutinizing all visitors who pass between the huge columns into the main piazza. Before such intrusions into Bernini's elegant architectural space, this was a well-beaten path for circulating nuns and priests, hurrying with serious intent to appointments with higher authorities. Just over the river in the Campo dei Fiori, the stern hooded figure of Giordano Bruno is a grim reminder of the fate awaiting those who incurred the wrath of the Church. In 1600 this monk, astronomer and philosopher was burnt at the stake here for heresy, largely for insisting that the earth moved around the sun.

Since Roman times, the city has been a noisy, dirty, busy place, but it is always possible to find a quiet spot to consider the passage of time as day follows night repeatedly around the ancient stones. The *Isola Tiburtina*, surrounded by the seven hills of Rome, is one such spot. This is the place

Steps by San Pietro in Vincoli (page 138)
Known as the Salita dei Borgia, these steps descend under what was believed to have been the garden of Vanozza Cattanei, where the Duke of Gandia was murdered. This is also supposed to be the site where in 534 BC the Roman queen Tullia murdered her father, Servius Tullius, the sixth king of Rome, running her chariot over his body. Whatever happened here in past centuries, the stairs remain a mysterious, sinister place, a construction so massive its bricks and stones seem to merge back into the very rock whence they came.

Temple of Vesta, Forum Romana
The smooth creamy marble pavement of the Via Sacra as its passes the hallowed temple of Vesta reiterates the theme of roads, but here the journey is more spiritual than terrestrial. The Temple was one of the most sacred sites in Rome and housed the Eternal Flame, tended by the Vestal Virgins and symbolizing the perpetuity of the Roman state. The Temple was reassembled in the 1930s from fragments that had been scattered around the Forum.

where the Via Salaria once crossed the river to reach the centre of the city. Established as a centre of healing as far back as 293 BC, when the Aesculapius Temple was established, the island is now dominated by a hospital. The traffic can still be clearly heard and the sodium streets lights intrude into the gathering darkness, but as a winter dusk descends upon the island and the river rushes past to its next port of call, washing the ancient crumbling stones of the Ponte Rotto on its way, it is just possible to hear only the noise of the water and to see little more than the silhouettes of the rooftops and trees. At such moments one might be living in any one of the many centuries that have passed since Romulus and Remus were suckled by the mythical she-wolf.

In the end, many visitors to Rome have left with a "love-hate" feeling towards the great city. It may be the constant noise, the insistence of beggars, the intrusive traffic, the inevitable overdose of culture, or just the overwhelming weight of history, but negative feelings are usually outweighed by the positive ones. The early American visitor Nathaniel Hawthorne commented after leaving the place that "hating her with all our might . . . we are astonished by the discovery, by and by, that our heartstrings have mysteriously attached themselves to the Eternal City, and are drawing us thitherward again, as if it were more familiar, more intimately our home, than even the spot where we were born." I often used to feel ambivalent about Rome, especially after over-energetic visits to photograph dozens of churches in a single week, trying to negotiate with obstinate bureaucracy for permission to photograph a particular building, having my cameras and film stolen and always having my appreciation of the place disturbed by bands of gypsy pickpockets. Now, all negative feelings have ebbed away. I stand entirely in awe of this centre of the civilized world. Reflecting on the people, work and ideas that flowed out of Rome, one develops a fuller understanding of all that returned to the Eternal City to glorify the stones on which the Empire was built; and an appreciation of the routes that transported all these people, their ideas, dreams and ambitions.

Clivus Capitolinus
Once a triumphal route for victorious generals, this steep road leads up to the Capitoline. Day after day the feet of tourists pound the massive stones as they end their visit to the Roman Forum.

San Giovanni in Laterano
Passing from shadow into light, the familiar
figure of a priest enters the hallowed space of
Rome's official cathedral as his predecessors
have done every day since the church was first
established in this spot by Constantine in the
fourth century AD.

Via Condotti
The Via del Corso follows the line of the Via
Flaminia as it proceeds from the Forum towards
the Porta Flaminia. Off this road are countless
side streets, one of the most notable being Via
Condotti, paradise for those dedicated to the art
of shopping.

Piazza San Pietro
Only a sudden rainstorm enables the visitor to
the Vatican to witness the main piazza virtually
empty at the height of summer. Two priests
linger by the fountain, perhaps still spellbound
and awestruck by the object of their pilgrimage
from the obscure provinces – the vast basilica of
San Pietro. The summer shower seems to have
washed away any last trace of colour from the
scene, leaving just the bare outlines of the priests
to mingle with Carlo Maderno's seventeenth-
century statuary topping the façade, and their
umbrellas to echo the piazza's fountains.

Piazza di Spagna

Just east from the Via Flaminia stand the early-
eighteenth-century steps now known as the
Spanish Steps, for long a centre for passionate
pilgrims visiting the city; in warm weather the
steps are crowded for much of the day and night.
Inside Keats' house to the right of the steps is a
list of names of writers who made their way here,
Hawthorne, James, Melville, Dickens, Eliot and
others, but the main literary association is with
Keats, who died of consumption here in 1821 at
the age of twenty-five.

Isola Tiburtina
As a winter dusk descends upon the island and the river rushes past to its next port of call, washing the ancient crumbling stones of the Ponte Rotto, it is possible to imagine oneself to be living in any of the many centuries that have passed in the history of the Eternal City.

Casa Manilio

This building was named after its humanist owner Lorenzo Manilio, who built the town house in 1468 and embellished it with architectural fragments he collected from the ancient sites of the city. The layers of time have been further complicated by engraved Latin and Greek texts that look as if they were also plundered from classical ruins, but which were, in fact, contemporary references to the owner.

Campidoglio
The mythical figures of Romulus and Remus
being suckled by the she-wolf are to be seen all
over Rome, often accompanied by the letters
SPQR, for Senatus Populusque Romanus – the
Senate and People of Rome. Here latter-day
custodians of the law pass the time of day on the
Capitol, Rome's ancient seat of government.

FURTHER READING

Bentley, James, and John Heseltine, *Rome* (George Philip, London, 1991)

Brosses, Charles de, *Familiar Letters Written in Italy in 1739–40*, from Claude Moatti, *The Search for Ancient Rome* (Thames and Hudson, London, 1993)

Cellini, Benvenuto, *The Life of Benvenuto Cellini*, first published 1728, revised nineteenth-century Roscoe translation (Oxford University Press, 1961)

Dickens, Charles, *Pictures from Italy*, first published 1888 (Penguin, London, 1998)

Goethe, J.W. von, *Italian Journey*, 1786–88, translated by W.H. Auden and Elizabeth Mayer (Penguin, London, 1992)

Hagen Victor von, *The Roads that Led to Rome* (Weidenfeld and Nicolson, London, 1967)

Hare, Augustus, *Walks in Rome*, first published 1871 (George Routledge and Sons, London)

Hawthorne, Nathaniel, passages on Rome from the *French and Italian Notebooks*, edited by his widow, 1883 edition, sourced online at: http://www.gutenberg.org/etext/7881

James, Henry, *Italian Hours*, first published 1909 (The Grove Press, New York, 1989)

Lawrence, D.H., *Etruscan Places*, first published 1932 (from *D.H. Lawrence and Italy*, Penguin, London, 1997)

Levi, Carlo, *Christ Stopped at Eboli*, first published 1945 (Quartet Books, London, 1997)

Fleeting Rome (John Wiley, New York, 2004)

Masson, Georgina, *Companion Guide to Rome* (Collins, London, 1986)

Montaigne, *Diaries*, first published 1581; *The Diary of Montaigne's Journey to Italy in 1580 and 1581*, translated by E.J. Trechmann. (Hogarth Press, London, 1929)

Roads to Rome: From Pisa, Bologna and Ravenna to the Eternal City (Thames and Hudson, London, 1958)

Staccioli, Romolo A., *The Roads of the Romans* (J. Paul Getty Museum, Los Angeles, 2003)

Strathern, Paul *The Medici* (Pimlico, 2005)

Thayer, Bill, *Lacus Curtius* website: http://penelope.uchicago.edu/Thayer/E/Roman/home.html.

Vasari, Giorgio, *The Lives of Painters, Sculptors and Architects* (Dent, London, 1963)

ACKNOWLEDGMENTS

I am indebted to Susan Berry for seeing the potential of this apparently obscure project and for making sure it found its way into print. I would also like to thank John Nicoll of Frances Lincoln Publishers and Chris Hudson of the Getty Museum for committing themselves to the idea before it was developed into a cogent form. Anne Wilson's creative flair for typography and supremely elegant design have made a major contribution, for which I am most grateful. I also very much appreciate the invaluable help and enthusiasm of Jo Christian, Kim Oliver, Caterina Favaretto and Sue Gladstone at Frances Lincoln Publishers. A special thanks to Colin Ford, not only for his thought-provoking foreword but also for his helpful advice on picture editing and his stimulating company on our walk together along the Via Appia outside Rome. It was a privilege to be able to share some of the experiences of such a notable figure in the world of photography. I should also like to register my gratitude to Alessio Colonnelli, who helped give me an insight into the view of younger Italians as well as correcting my mistakes and producing a sympathetic translation into Italian. I am grateful for the support of Luca Magni of Baglioni Hotels, whose keen interest in the visual arts led to his offering me the comfortable hospitality of the Regina Hotel Baglioni in Rome while I completed the project.

John Heseltine

RIGHT: *Trajan's Column*
This famous marble column 130 feet (40 metres)
high uses 2,500 intricately carved figures to relate
the history of Trajan's campaign against the Dacians
of Romania between AD 101 and 106.

OVERLEAF: *Goalpost*
The empty and desolate landscape of the Piano
Grande in the Sibillini Mountains near Castelluccio
looks more like a mountainous Tibetan desert than
an Italian landscape. It is a surprising place to find a
football pitch.

ENDPAPERS, FRONT: *La Storta*
The Via Cassia's early progress away from Rome
passes through a residential area that is
unremarkable in character – except for glimpses of
layers of political history read in peeling posters.

ENDPAPERS, BACK: *Carsulae*
The passage of time is expressed in well-worn ruts
in the original surface of the Via Flaminia on its
northern approach to the ruined Roman city of
Carsulae in modern Umbria.